COMING HOME

Glen Abbey Book Collection

A Reference Guide to the Big Book of Alcoholics Anonymous

by Stewart C.
ISBN: 0-934125-01-5
Price: $9.95

A Year to Remember

52 Contemplative Messages on 12 step Recovery and Christianity

by Reverend Bruce
Van Blair
ISBN:0-934125-05-8
Price: $8.95

Stepping Stones to Recovery

Spiritual Insights into Recovery Compiled from the Membership of Alcoholics Anonymous over the past Fifty Years

by Bill Pittman
ISBN: 0-934125-04-X
Price: $8.95

A A The Way It Began

by Bill Pittman
ISBN: 0-934125-02-3
Price: $7.95

Glen Abbey Books
PO Box 19762
Seattle WA 98109
1-800-782-2239
(206) 284-4603

Adult Children of Alcoholics
Coming Home

By Peggy King Anderson

Published by Glen Abbey Books
PO Box 19762
Seattle, WA 98109
1-800-782-2239

Printed and bound in the United States of America

First Edition

Library of Congress Catalog Card Number
87 - 73388

Includes Book List
ISBN 0-934125-06-6

ACKNOWLEDGEMENTS

This book has been a gift to me - not only the gift of its own creation, but also a gift of the many wonderful people it has brought into my life. I would like to thank especially Julie Rusk, the dedicated R. N. from Kirkland CareUnit, who led me practically by the hand to the various people and groups I needed to meet for the writing of this book. In addition, she gave many hours of her time in reading and critiquing the various stages of **Coming Home** and for this I will be forever thankful.

It was Julie who brought me to the Kirkland Morning Study Group, and also to the Sunday Englewood Al-Atot Group. Thanks to the adults and children in these two groups whose generous sharing helped to shape this book. My special thanks to Jim, who gave me some key advice at the very inception of the book.

I appreciate also the several counselors who generously agreed to review the finished book - Lorie Dwinnell, Sally Hartley, Marcelle Vadhelm, among others.

I thank Pat Moriarty, my publisher, for his charismatic insight that kept me on target in the final vision of this book. I want to thank also my editor, Ciaran O'Mahony. He has been always both kind and wise in his guidance to me, and for this I am deeply grateful.

I have one special gift that many writers do not have: my very own Tuesday Morning Writing Support Group. Thank you Cathy, Nancy, Pat, Jody, Chris, Jan, Dawn. On days when I wanted to quietly crawl into a hole and forget this entire project, your gentle nagging and loving encouragement kept me going.

And finally, I thank my family, who patiently ate soup and sandwiches many a night when deadlines beckoned.

I pray that many thousands may be touched by this book, which all of you have made possible.

Preface

If you are an adult, you may be surprised when you turn to page one of this book. This is a children's story. But before you give it to a child to read, do something for yourself. Read this book. Read it for the unhealed child within you.

If you've been involved in ACOA at all, you know that one of the most important steps in your healing is going back to the feelings you shut off as a child, and becoming aware of them so that you can step beyond into freedom. This is a step into healing.

Dedication

To my husband Ken, who believed in me.

PKA

.

To those who trusted, even when they didn't understand.

NED

Table of Contents

Chapter 1

A Home For Molly And Bubbles

Jenny Turner caught her breath as she walked into the kitchen. Brian had the fishbowl balanced on the edge of the counter and he was standing on tiptoe, edging it over to the rim of the sink.

"Brian! What are you doing? I told you I'd help you clean that before supper."

Brian's face had an all too familiar frown on it. "Molly and Bubbles got scared. They can't breathe with

1

all that yuck in their bowl. I called you twice, but you didn't answer."

Jenny got out the small net from the corner drawer. "I'm sorry, Brian. I started to draw, and I guess I wasn't listening." She leaned over the bowl. "How does this water get dirty so fast? I just cleaned it Saturday."

"The fishbowl's too little. Daddy says he'll take me this afternoon to get a big aquarium for them. It'll have a pump and everything. He promised."

Jenny pressed her lips together. She scooped Molly and Bubbles out and plopped them into a jar full of fresh water. Her father and his promises. When would Brian realize what she'd found out long ago? Their father never kept promises.

"Where IS Daddy?" she asked.

Brian shrugged his shoulders. "He went to see about a job this morning. Mom said he'd be back before I got home from school."

His face brightened. "Maybe he got the job, and he had to start work. Then when he comes home he'll be so happy that we'll get colored rocks for the bottom of the aquarium, and one of those little divers that makes bubbles."

"You haven't even got the aquarium yet," Jenny said. There was the sound of screeching brakes out front and she looked out the window over the sink. A yellow cab had just stopped in front of the house. The cab door opened and her father got out. Jenny stood frozen, watching as he fumbled in his pocket, then shoved a handful of bills at the driver.

Coming Home

Jenny stood frozen, watching as he fumbled in his pocket, then shoved a handful of bills at the driver.

Hastily she dumped the fish into the bowl of clean water. "Come on, Brian. Let's go upstairs. Daddy's home."

He squirmed as she grabbed his sleeve. "I don't want to go upstairs. Besides, Daddy was in a good mood this morning."

"He doesn't have the car. He must have left it downtown."

Brian was silent. Even he knew what it meant when their father came home in a cab. "He's drinking again. He promised he wouldn't."

Jenny put the net back in the drawer and hastily wiped the spilled water off the countertop. When her father came home this way, any little thing could set him off. She remembered how angry he'd gotten two weeks ago after he'd gone for the other job interview.

She'd thought he was going to hit her that day for sure.

There was a clatter from the front yard, and then a loud bang. He must have fallen over the lawn chair. Her hands were shaking. She held on to the edge of the counter. "Come on, Brian. I'll teach you how to draw a horse." She tried to keep her voice from trembling. She took a quick look out the window. Her father was coming up the sidewalk now, moving carefully.

Brian turned his back to the window. He stood stubbornly, his hands around the edge of the fishbowl. "I don't want to draw a horse. I like to draw trucks."

"Okay, okay," Jenny said. "I'll show you how to draw a diesel truck. Hurry up, though." She pushed the fishbowl to the back of the counter and grabbed Brian's hand. He scowled and pulled away from her. Then his face crumpled, and he looked like he was going to cry. "All right. I'm coming."

Jenny hurried up the stairs. She couldn't hear her father yet. He must still be making his way up the sidewalk. She hoped he wouldn't fall asleep out in the front yard. He'd done that last time, and Mrs. Pearson next door had told everyone about it. It had been hard on Brian; Kevin Pearson was in his second grade class. When they got to the top of the stairs, Brian stopped. He leaned over the railing, looking down into the kitchen. He sighed. "I'll never have an aquarium for Molly and Bubbles, will I?"

Jenny put her hand on his shoulder. The lump in her throat felt too big for her to say anything.

Brian kicked the railing. "I hate Daddy. My fish will never have a good place to live, and it's all his fault."

The front door flew open. It smashed against the wall, knocking a picture to the floor.

"Quick, Brian," Jenny said. She pulled him into her bedroom and shut the door.

Chapter 2

Why Do We Always Pretend?

Jenny stood for a moment, her breath coming in little gasps. She could hear her father mutter as he made his way through the living room. There was a loud crash and the sound of muffled cursing.

Jenny turned the lock on the door. Brian sat on the bed watching her. His eyes looked dark in his pale face and his freckles stood out.

It was quiet downstairs now. Jenny listened, then went over to her desk. She pulled out a pad of drawing paper and picked up her pastels. "Look, Brian. I'll show you how to mix the colors so the truck looks like it's moving."

She didn't know how she could talk when she had such a big lump in her throat, but somehow her voice came out. When she first put the colored stick against the paper, her hand shook and the line almost went off the edge.

We're safe. We're safe in here, she thought.

But she felt trapped.

She closed her eyes and took deep breaths to calm herself. She had a game she played at times like this. She imagined she was in a beautiful garden, far away from here. The garden had a waterfall and green ferns, and a patch of blue and white daisies. If she thought about it hard enough, it always calmed her down inside.

She opened her eyes and looked at the wavering line on the paper in front of her. She tried again, and this time the lines of the truck were steady.

Brian sat on the bed. He still hadn't said anything. She got up and went over to him. "It's okay, Brian. I think he went to sleep. Come on. I'll show you how to put racing stripes on your diesel."

"Diesels don't have racing stripes," Brian said. "And I don't like those chalk things to draw with." But he stood up and followed her over to the desk. Jenny took out a set of markers, and watched while Brian drew the wobbly lines of a red truck. "That's good, Brian." Her brother was intent now, biting the edge of his lip as he sketched. He looked just like Daddy when he did that.

She had a sudden memory of her father sitting beside her when she was little, guiding her hand as he showed her how to draw a horse. She felt her eyes sting and quickly stood up. She looked at Brian. I won't cry, she thought.

Faintly, from downstairs, she heard the front door open and close. She listened.

She could hear her mother in the kitchen, putting away groceries. Then she heard voices, her mother's low and angry, her father's loud. She couldn't hear what they were saying without opening the door and she didn't want to do that.

Brian sat at the desk, his back to the door, but she saw that he had stopped drawing. His hands were frozen in position, the purple marker just above one crooked wheel. The voices got louder. The front door slammed.

This was how it always was. He'd be gone for a few hours, then sometime in the night he'd come back. She heard her mother's footsteps outside in the hall. "Jenny? Are you okay? Is Brian in there with you?"

Jenny unlocked the door. Her mother's face looked tired. "Are you two hungry? I thought maybe we could go out for hamburgers or something."

Why do we always pretend? Jenny thought. We act like nothing's wrong, even when there's broken furniture in the living room and

Brian and I are locked in the bedroom when she gets home.

"Where's Daddy?" Brian asked.

Her mother didn't say anything for a minute. She looked at Brian's face, then into Jenny's eyes. Jenny saw an expression on her mother's face she hadn't seen before -- a hard, determined look. It scared her.

Her mother led them over to the bed and sat down, an arm around each of them. Jenny felt her heart pounding even before her mother spoke the words.

"I don't know where Daddy is now, Brian. I told him to leave and this time I told him he can't come back until he gets treatment."

"No!" Brian said. "You can't make him go. He promised to get an aquarium for my fish." He pulled away from her and ran from the room. Seconds later Jenny heard his bedroom door slam shut.

Her mother didn't say anything for a moment. Then she sighed and stood up. "I'll go get some hamburgers. I'll be back in a few minutes."

Chapter 3

Daddy Has a Problem

Jenny turned her pillow over and tried to get into a comfortable position. It was almost midnight, but she couldn't get to sleep. Her father was gone and he wasn't coming back -- that's what her mother said.

Jenny knew he would never go for treatment. Even if he did he wouldn't stick it out.

The room next to her was quiet; she hoped Brian wouldn't have nightmares again. He tried to act so tough, but she knew he had cried himself to sleep. He wouldn't eat dinner, even though their mom had brought back quarter pounders with cheese for them.

Jenny sighed and shifted her feet, trying to find a cool spot at the foot of the bed.

Would her father come back? And if he didn't, was it her fault? It seemed as if everything he yelled about lately was something she'd done wrong; yesterday it was her drawing pad and pastels left out on the dining room table. Sometimes she felt as if she were to blame for his drinking.

She kept listening for the sound of the front door.

She could hear the soft shush-shush of her mother's slippers pacing in the bedroom at the end of the hall. Maybe she was sorry for what she'd said this afternoon. She was always changing her mind about things, especially when she was upset.

And would her father even remember what had happened?

Sometimes -- lots of times lately -- he forgot things.

Jenny stared out the window at the streetlight. Hundreds of tiny moths fluttered around it, just like the mixed-up thoughts in her head.

When had her father started drinking too much? When had he started forgetting things? When she'd been little, they'd been such a happy family. She remembered picnics, and going to the zoo, riding on her father's shoulders to see the elephants better.

Did Brian have any happy memories? It seemed as if the problems had started when he was a baby. Maybe it was Brian's fault; from the time he was little he'd been getting into things. No, that didn't seem right. Her father hardly ever got mad at Brian.

She was getting a headache. The thoughts inside her were bumping together, like the moths outside under the street light. It was too hard to figure out when it had started or what was going to happen next. She turned her pillow over again, and kicked off the extra blanket. Finally she fell into a restless sleep.

When she woke up in the morning her stomach hurt. She got dressed and went down to the family room.

The couch was empty. Her father hadn't come home. Her mother's eyes were puffy when she came down to breakfast, but all she said was, "Jenny, could you pick up some milk this afternoon on your way home from school? We're almost out."

When Jenny came home that afternoon, carrying the carton of milk, she opened the front door cautiously. Maybe her father had come home while she was at school. Part of her hoped he had -- but she still felt relieved when the house was quiet.

She walked into the kitchen. The dishes were stacked neatly in the sink where she'd put them this morning after breakfast. Brian was standing at the counter, tracing his finger listlessly around the edge of the fishbowl. "Daddy didn't come home last night," he said.

Jenny didn't say anything. Brian dumped a handful of fish flakes into the bowl.

"Not so much!" Jenny said. "They'll get sick."

Brian scowled. "I'm just trying to cheer them up. They're sad today." He put the box of fish food back in the drawer and leaned his chin on his hand, watching the fish.

Jenny put the milk in the refrigerator and took out an apple. Brian straightened up. "I know! I'll put something in their bowl to make them happy. I'll get one of my matchbox cars, or maybe a Star Wars guy."

Jenny shook her head. "That's not a good idea, Brian. How about some marbles instead?"

"Okay. I've got some in the drawer with my baseball cards. I'll go get them." He smiled and ran up the stairs, two at a time. Jenny watched, feeling a little sad. Brian's smile used to light up his whole face, but lately he hardly smiled at all.

She wandered into the living room. The magazines that her father had thrown were neatly stacked now underneath the coffee table. The telltale page of one that her mother had missed stuck out from under the edge of the couch.

There was an empty space on the end table where her mother's favorite porcelain lamp had been. That must have been the crash she'd heard just before she'd locked her bedroom door.

She heard Brian's footsteps and went back into the kitchen. He was down on his hands and knees hunting in the cupboard. "Maybe we could put Molly and Bubbles in the mixing bowl, Jenny. Then they'd have more room."

"Mom wouldn't appreciate that. Besides, it's not big enough to make much difference."

Brian closed the cupboard door slowly. "Well anyway, I've got the marbles. I brought mostly blue ones. Fish like blue best. But I brought some red ones too."

Jenny smiled. "Well we'd better wash all of them off before we put them in the bowl. It looks as if you were eating a peanut butter and jelly sandwich the last time you played with them." She put soapy water in a pan to wash the marbles. "While I'm doing this, why don't you set out some fresh water for next time, Brian."

He filled the jar with water from the faucet and stood on tiptoe to push it to the very back of the counter.

"That's so Mom won't forget and throw the water out again," he said.

Jenny nodded and rinsed the marbles, then put them into the bowl she had just cleaned.

"Let me put Molly and Bubbles back in," Brian said. He carefully transferred the fish and watched as they swam in little circles, bumping the marbles curiously. The front door opened.

"Jenny? Brian?" Mom walked into the kitchen. Jenny knew immediately that something had happened. Her mother was smiling.

"Daddy checked into an alcohol treatment center today. They called

Coming Home

"Daddy checked into an alcohol treatment center today."

me at work to get the information they needed."

Brian looked up at her, a frown on his face. "What's that mean? I want him to come home."

"It means that Daddy's finally admitted he has a problem, Brian. It means that people who know what they're doing can help him get well. He'll be at the treatment center about four weeks but I think we can see him for a short visit before that."

"What about the other time?" Jenny said. She felt her fingernails digging into her palms and realized she had her hands clenched. That time two years ago; that was when her father had been fired. He'd checked himself into a treatment center then too -- but he'd left after just a few hours. He'd gone on a drinking spree and had broken her favorite clock, the one with the glass chimes.

Her mother was silent.

Jenny picked her schoolbag up off the table. "I'm going up to my room."

"How about a snack? I brought home some cookies. Raspberry filled -- your favorite."

"No thanks," Jenny said. "I'm not hungry. And besides I have a lot of homework."

She turned and walked out of the room. He wouldn't stay this time either.

Why couldn't her mother see that?

Chapter 4

Too Busy for Soccer

Wednesday and Thursday dragged by. "Is Daddy still there?" Brian asked. "At that treatment center?"

Her mother nodded, but didn't say anything more. She seemed tired. Brian frowned, and went back to drawing a picture of Molly and Bubbles. In his drawing, they were in a gigantic bowl that filled the whole page.

Jenny didn't ask her mother any questions. She didn't want to hear the answers -- or the silence.

At school it was hard to concentrate. She couldn't make herself think about fractions when she didn't know if she'd ever see her father again.

On Friday morning she sat at her desk waiting for the recess bell to ring. Mrs. Neven's voice droned on about common denominators, while Jenny doodled in the margins of her paper. She realized suddenly what she had drawn, and quickly folded the paper in half. She felt her cheeks getting warm.

She had sketched the outline of her father, a bottle in his hand.

She looked around to see if anyone had noticed. Marcie Williams, in the desk across from her, smiled a friendly smile. Jenny crumpled the paper and shoved it into her pocket just as the bell rang.

Marcie caught her eye. "See you outside," she said. Jenny was surprised. She'd sometimes wished she and Marcie could be friends, but it hadn't happened so far. It was hard to make friends, the way things were at home.

She stood up to follow Marcie outside but Mrs. Neven put a hand on her shoulder. "Stay for a minute, Jenny. I'd like to talk to you."

Jenny's heart started to pound as she sat back down at her desk. Could Mrs. Neven have seen the doodles? She waited anxiously while the rest of the students hurried out to the playground.

Mrs. Neven leaned against a desk. "All right, Jenny," she said. "What's going on? You're usually a good student, but your grades have been down all week."

She hadn't seen the drawing then. Jenny's legs felt weak with relief. "I -- guess I just haven't been trying hard enough. Maybe I could do some extra credit work."

Mrs. Neven shook her head. "I don't think that's the answer. You seem distracted, Jenny. Are you sure nothing's wrong?"

She swallowed. For just a moment she wondered what Mrs. Neven would say if she told her the truth:

I'm worried that my father may never come back. Or maybe I'm worried that he will come back, and shout at my mother and break the lamps in our living room and fall asleep on our front lawn when he's drinking too much.

But she didn't say it.

Mrs. Neven was still watching her with concerned eyes. "Parent teacher conferences are in two weeks, Jenny. I'd like to talk to your mom and dad then."

Trapped. Jenny hated this feeling. "My father... My father's on a business trip. I'm not sure if he'll be back."

Mrs. Neven nodded. "I'll plan to see your mother then. Jenny, I hope you'll let me know if there's anything I can do."

Jenny stood up, working hard to fight the tears that threatened to start any minute. She hurried out to the playground before her teacher could ask more questions. Standing in the sunshine, she took deep breaths.

She imagined herself in her special garden, with beautiful ferns growing by the waterfall. She would be sitting on a rock by the daisies, sketching them.

"Hey, Jenny!"

She jumped at the sound of Marcie's voice. "Come on over and play with us. We're just about to start a game of double-dutch."

But Carolyn, who was turning the rope, made a face and turned her back on Jenny. "It's your turn, Marcie. Jump in," she called out impatiently. Jenny sighed and walked over toward the ball field.

Kevin Pearson and her brother Brian were standing at the edge of the field arguing. Jenny moved closer. "So what?" Brian was shouting. "My father's too busy to come to the soccer games."

Kevin laughed. "Yeah, busy doing what? He hasn't even come to one game."

Brian's face was red and his hands clenched into fists. "My dad plays on a REAL soccer team," Brian shouted. "That's why he can't come. He plays for -- for the Sounders!"

"Come off it, Brian Turner! My mom told me about your dad. Your dad's a drunk!"

Brian's fist shot out and caught Kevin on the shoulder, sending him sprawling. Jenny rushed forward and grabbed Brian's arm, just as Kevin scrambled to his feet and ran. Brian lunged after him, but Jenny hung on to his shirt. Her brother's face was twisted with anger, and the furious look reminded her again of her father -- her father when he'd been drinking.

Coming Home

"Come off it, Brian Turner! My mom told me about your dad. Your dad's a drunk!"

Her hand started shaking. She'd seen that same look on her father's face a few weeks ago, when he'd kicked her bike over in the front yard. She'd made the mistake of leaving it on the sidewalk, and her father had tripped over it on his way in. He'd been so angry he'd kept kicking until the rim of the front wheel was bent.

Brian had stopped struggling now. She let go of his shirt and he stood in front of her defiantly. She took a deep breath but still her voice came out shaky. "Why do you let him bother you, Brian? Why don't you just walk away?"

Brian scowled back at her, but she saw the tears shining in his eyes. "I hate him. Why does he keep saying Dad's a drunk?"

He is a drunk, Jenny thought. Our dad is a drunk. She swallowed hard. "Kevin's just dumb, Brian. You can't let him get to you."

A couple of tears had slipped out now, and Brian wiped them away furiously, leaving dark streaks of mud on his face. "When will Dad get home from that treatment center? I only have two more soccer games, and I want him to come."

Jenny sighed. "Brian, Dad never goes to your games, even when he's home."

"Mom said things are going to be different now," Brian said. "She said Dad's getting better, and he won't drink anymore. I think he might get an aquarium for Molly and Bubbles pretty soon."

Jenny's head was pounding. "You'd better go wash your face," she said.

Brian stood there stubbornly, his fists still clenched, a spot of mud on his shirt.

"Come on," she said more gently. She led him over to the drinking fountain, and took a crumpled Kleenex out of her pocket. She washed his face, and tried to scrub the muddy spot from his shirt.

The bell rang. Jenny gave Brian's shoulder a squeeze. "I have to go," she said. "I don't want to be late for class. You'd better go too. I'll see you at home after school."

But when she looked back from the door of the building, Brian was still standing by the drinking fountain. As she watched, he gave the wall a savage kick, then turned and trudged toward the second grade classroom.

Chapter 5

The Strawberry Roan

When Jenny walked out of the classroom at three, she saw Marcie hurrying toward her from the art room. "Wait up, Jenny. I'll walk with you."

Jenny waited, pleased, but also a little uneasy.

"Why did you walk away when I asked you to play at recess?" Marcie asked.

Jenny looked away. "There were too many people playing already." The load of books she was carrying

41

shifted. The folder on top slid to the ground, spilling papers out on the hall floor. As she bent over to get them, the rest of her books fell.

Couldn't she do anything right?

"I'll help," Marcie said, and scrambled after the scattered books. A sudden breeze from the door picked up one of the sketches and it sailed into the air. "Got it!" Marcie said. She grabbed the sketch and stood looking at it for several moments. It was a drawing Jenny had done of a strawberry roan.

"Jenny, this is good! How did you learn to do this?"

A memory came back to her, of her father sitting at an easel by the side of the road. He was sketching the flowing lines of the horse in the nearby pasture. She was standing beside him, watching his every move. She'd thought her father was wonderful when she was four years old.

She sighed and shrugged her shoulders. "I've just always liked to draw."

Marcie was looking at the other pictures now. "These are all good. I wish I could draw like this."

Jenny spoke quickly to push away the memories that were crowding into her mind. "I could teach you how to sketch if you want. It's not hard to draw a horse."

Marcie's face lit up. "I'd love it. I'd invite you over to my house this afternoon, but it's wild there. I have three little brothers and my mom runs a daycare center besides." She made a face. "It's always noisy."

Carefully she slipped the drawings back into the folder and handed them to Jenny. The two girls walked outside and started down the sidewalk. "Maybe I could come over to your house some day after school and you could teach me," Marcie said.

Here it was again; the reason why it was so hard for her to have friends. For a moment she didn't say anything. "I'll check," she said finally.

Marcie grinned. "Great! Well, see you later. I turn off here."

Jenny stood watching as Marcie ran toward the bus stop. It must be nice having a normal family, even if there were a lot of kids. She bet Marcie never felt lonely.

Jenny continued on her way, walking slowly. What would it be like, to be able to invite a friend over to the house -- to invite Marcie over?

She stopped walking suddenly.

She COULD invite Marcie to come over. Her father wasn't there. Maybe she could even invite Marcie to spend the night. She'd overheard conversations at school after friends had spent the night together. Carolyn Hampton and the others would giggle about the silly telephone calls, the late night milkshakes, the talking. She'd never been part of that world, but now... maybe she could have a taste of it.

She looked up, surprised to see she was only half a block from the house. Brian was walking toward her, looking down at something he carried carefully in both hands.

"Brian," she called.

His head jerked up and he quickly crossed his arms to hide what he was holding. She walked up to him. "Brian, what have you got?"

He had that stubborn look on his face again.

"Brian..." Jenny said gently. Reluctantly he held out his hands. She looked in disbelief at the Ziploc bag he was holding. Inside the bag, swimming in frantic little circles, were Molly and Bubbles.

"They don't like it in their bowl," he said.

Jenny didn't know whether to laugh or cry. She took the plastic bag from Brian's outstretched hands. "Why do you do these things, Brian? Those poor fish!

His head jerked up and he quickly crossed his arms to
hide what he was holding.

Come on, we'd better get them back where they belong."

"You were late getting home from school," Brian said. "They felt lonesome at the house with nobody there."

"Well I'm home now. Let's put them back in their bowl."

"Jenny, when does Daddy get to come home? My fish weren't lonesome when Daddy was here."

Jenny felt her temples throbbing. Did Brian really remember how it was when their father was at home? The fighting, the tension, her mother crying?

As if Brian was reading her mind, he said, "Sometimes it was fun. Sometimes Daddy read to me in the afternoon."

She hurried up the sidewalk and pushed open the front door. The house was silent. It had the stale muggy feeling of a house that had been shut up all day.

There was a note taped to the refrigerator:

Jenny,

I have an important meeting tonight; I'll explain later. Soup and sandwiches for dinner. Home about 9:30.

Love, Mom.

Jenny sighed as she helped Brian put Molly and Bubbles back in their bowl. Brian was right. The house did feel lonesome.

Chapter 6

What's a Normal Family Like?

Jenny was dozing when she heard her mother come in that night. She called out sleepily, and her mom walked into the bedroom. Jenny reached up for a hug. "Where were you?"

Her mother sat down. "I was at an Al-Anon meeting, honey." She pushed Jenny's hair back gently. "I found out a lot more about alcoholism tonight, and why Daddy acts the way he does. I also found out that there are some things that the rest of us in the family can do to feel better."

Just what she thought. Her mom was looking for some way to make it be okay, like she always did. Jenny pulled away from her.

"I'm thinking of taking you with me next Thursday. There's another meeting the same time as mine with several kids your age in it."

Jenny rolled over, turning away from her mother's questioning eyes. "I have too much homework to go anywhere at night."

"Jenny..."

"Please, Mom. I don't want to talk about it right now. I'm tired."

"All right. We'll talk about it later." Her mother kissed her and started out of the room. She paused by

"Please, Mom. I don't want to talk about it right now.
I'm tired."

the door. "How was the rest of your day?"

Suddenly Jenny remembered. She raised herself up on one elbow. "It was okay. Mom, would it be all right if I invite a friend to spend the night next weekend?"

She could feel her mother's delight across the darkened room. Her mom was always worrying about Jenny not having any friends. "That's fine, honey. Is she someone from your class?"

Jenny nodded. "Her name's Marcie."

"Well, let me know what night you settle on, and we can plan something special. We could have pizza for dinner if you want."

"That would be neat." This must be how normal families were.

Jenny could imagine Carolyn Hampton's mother talking to her just like that. Only in Carolyn's family, her father would be downstairs reading the paper. And when it was time for the party, Carolyn's father would offer to drive the girls down to Breyer's for ice cream after supper, and maybe a movie. She sighed and lay back down. "Good night, Mom."

Better to have her father gone than home. At least now she could make plans and know what to expect. She'd just tell Marcie her dad was on a business trip.

There was no one in the kitchen when Jenny came downstairs Monday morning. Her mother had the early shift cashiering, but Brian should be eating his breakfast by now. She saw a cereal bowl and a splatter of milk at his place. He must have eaten already.

She walked over to the counter to check Molly and Bubbles. Those two fish were survivors. They had to be with Brian around. As she got closer, she saw a brown tinge in the water. Molly and Bubbles were swimming at the very top of the bowl.

There was something in the bottom of the bowl; something besides marbles. She peered in. Rust spiraled up from the small diesel truck lying on its side.

"Oh, Brian," Jenny groaned. "Why can't you leave these poor fish alone?" She got the net out of the kitchen drawer.

"Did you call me?" Brian walked into the room, lugging his case of matchbox cars and Star War people.

"I told you not to put those cars in the fishbowl, Brian. Look at the rust. You're going to poison them. It's a good thing we set out fresh water last night to clean the bowl."

She scooped the two little fish out of the rusty water. Brian was quiet. Jenny looked over at him, surprised that he wasn't arguing. He watched while she finished cleaning the bowl. "Jenny?" Something was bothering him; she could tell by the look on his face. "Are you going to go to that meeting Thursday? Mom says we'll get better quicker if we all go."

Jenny's hand jerked and she almost dropped the fishbowl. "There's nothing wrong with US, Brian. Dad's the one who's got a problem."

"Mom says she feels better since she started going to Al-Anon meetings. She told me she went to one even before Daddy left."

"I'm not going to any meeting, Brian. You can go if you want." Jenny put the bowl back on the counter. "It's time to leave for school. Come on."

She saw Marcie getting off the bus when they turned onto Baker Street. Brian went on ahead while Jenny waited. Marcie waved and started running toward her.

She seems so confident, Jenny thought. Even though she complains about all the kids at home, she always seems so happy. It must be nice to have a normal family.

Out loud she said, "I asked my Mom, and you can spend the night this weekend if you want."

Marcie looked disappointed. "I can't, Jenny. I just found out last night I'll be gone all weekend. My uncle and aunt in Spokane are celebrating their 25th wedding anniversary with this big party. What about next weekend instead?"

"That sounds okay. How about Friday night?"

Marcie nodded. "I've got a box of games I'll bring over. Trying to play games at my house is almost impossible. There are hundreds of little kids running around all the time." Marcie rolled her eyes. "You can't believe how crazy it gets sometimes."

Jenny's stomach felt tight. Marcie didn't know what crazy was. All of a sudden she felt a familiar panic setting in. Usually when things got put off, they didn't work out at all.

She forced a smile onto her face. "Brian can be a pain sometimes too, but I'll tell him to leave us alone that night." She would act normal, and maybe everything would work out all right. If her father would just stay at the treatment center until Marcie had spent the night. That's all she asked: one day and one night when she could be like everyone else.

Chapter 7

Do Goldfish Know There's a God?

On Thursday evening, Jenny sat toying with the piece of chicken on her plate. "Mom, do you know yet when Dad's coming home?"

Her mother handed Brian a glass of milk, then turned to look at Jenny. "In three weeks, if he cooperates. It's possible he'll have one home visit before then."

"Do you think that would be before next weekend?" Her hand ached and she looked down, suddenly realizing how tightly she was holding her fork.

Her mother sighed. "I doubt it, Jenny. Your dad is having a hard time right now."

What did that mean? Was he drinking again already? She decided she didn't want to know. She took a bite of chicken and waited a minute before speaking. "Marcie will be gone this weekend, but she said she can spend the night a week from Friday."

Her mom smiled a tired smile. "Good. Make a list of what you'd like for treats, and I'll pick some up when I do the shopping."

"What about me?" Brian asked. "I want to pick out a treat too. I want banana popsicles."

"We can get some on the way home from the meeting tonight," her mom said. She turned to Jenny. "Are you sure you wouldn't like to go with us? These people know what they're talking about. You'll be amazed at how much better you'll feel if you go."

Not again. Jenny felt a rush of anger but she pushed it down inside. "I feel fine. I told you, Mom; I've had a lot of homework lately."

It was true. She was doing extra work each night now, so that Mrs. Neven wouldn't say anything else about her falling behind.

She cut a minute piece of chicken and took a long time chewing and swallowing it.

Brian helped himself to a scoop of mashed potatoes. "They have cookies after the meetings. And

Mom says there's lots of kids our age."

Jenny stood up and pushed her chair in.

She tried to ignore the disappointed look on her mother's face as she hurried out of the room. Brian's voice trailed after her. "Guess what else, Jenny? We get to stop at the pet store on the way and look at aquariums."

The last thing she heard before she went up the stairs was her mother's voice. "I said we'd LOOK at them, Brian. We can't afford to get one right now."

Then why are we spending so much for the treatment center? Jenny thought.

You'd think her mother would realize what a waste of money THAT was.

* * * * * * *

Marcie seemed excited when she hurried up to Jenny the next morning at recess. "I brought this for you to look at. Don't laugh now." She handed her a yellow folder with papers poking out in every direction. "These are some of the things I've done. I practice every time I get a chance, but somehow, my horses don't look anything like yours."

Jenny pulled a picture out of the folder. She smiled as she looked at the fat brown horse with a head too big for his body. Marcie had a lot to learn about proportions, but there was something appealing about her drawing anyway. The horse was leaping over a brightly colored planet that hung in a deep blue sky.

"I like it," she said.

Marcie made a face. "I know it's not right, but I don't know how to fix it."

"Here, I'll show you." Jenny sat down on the bench by the building and quickly sketched a copy of Marcie's horse, lengthening the neck and the legs.

"So that's what was wrong. Let me try." Marcie pulled a pencil out of her bookbag.

The loud clang of the first bell interrupted them. Marcie made a face. "I think I've got the idea. I'll practice and when we go over to your house next Friday we can have a marathon drawing lesson." She grinned. "Stick with me, Jenny.

When I'm rich and famous, I'll give you all the credit."

Jenny felt warm inside. The loneliness she felt so often was gone for the moment. Marcie liked her.

"Isn't that your brother sitting on the bench?" Marcie asked.

Jenny made a face. "I'll bet he didn't even notice the warning bell." She walked over to Brian.

Marcie followed. She leaned over to look at the paper beside him on the bench. "What are you drawing, Brian? Are you an artist too?"

Brian held up the paper and Jenny sighed. It was a picture of Molly and Bubbles swimming happily around a very large aquarium; a copy of the same picture he'd been drawing all week.

Coming Home

It was a picture of Molly and Bubbles swimming happily around a very large aquarium.

"That's really neat," Marcie said. "Okay, Brian, I'll tell you a goldfish joke. There are these two fish swimming around in their bowl, and one says to the other, By golly, now I'm sure there's a God. How do you know that for sure? the other fish asks. Well, silly, the first fish says, who do you think sprinkles food in our bowl every day?"

Brian looked puzzled and Marcie grinned. "Okay, so it wasn't that great a joke. Do you have goldfish, Brian?"

He nodded. "But their bowl's too little. I saw this one at the fish store last night. Mom said it costs too much."

Jenny interrupted. "You'd better get moving, Brian. You're going to be late for class again."

He scowled at her, but he got up reluctantly and started for his classroom.

"Hey, Brian," Marcie called after him. "Don't be discouraged. If you want something enough, you usually get it eventually."

Sure, Jenny thought. Sure.

Chapter 8

Disaster Strikes

The following Wednesday, just as Jenny was taking a pan of homemade macaroni and cheese out of the oven, her mother walked in from work. She had a strange look on her face; Jenny couldn't tell if she was happy or upset.

"Dad gets to come home Friday afternoon for a six hour visit," she said.

Jenny stood frozen, holding the macaroni and cheese in front of her. She could feel her hands burning from the heat, even through the potholders. She set the pan down on top of the stove.

"What about Marcie?" she asked.

Her mother looked at her. "Oh, Jenny. I forgot. They gave Dad the pass for Friday because I work Saturday and Sunday this week."

She set a bag of groceries down on the counter. "Do you think Marcie could come Saturday night instead? If she can't, keep it the way it is. We can't always be changing plans just because of Dad."

Her mother was watching her face. "Jenny, it will be okay. Your dad's working hard on his twelve steps and the rest of the program. You'll be surprised when you see him."

"Twelve steps?" Jenny said. Her voice sounded hoarse to her.

"I forgot you don't know about that," her mother said. "You haven't gone to the meetings. It's part of Dad's program, principles to help him get well. He's doing a lot better now."

"Just a few days ago you said he wasn't cooperating at all."

"Well now he is," her mother said shortly, and walked out of the kitchen. Jenny sighed. Her mother always saw things the way she wanted to. There was no way her father would really stop drinking. If he didn't drink now, he'd drink next week -- or the week after that. Then he'd get angry again, and throw things and yell at all of them.

Her father was the one who made life miserable for her. So why did she always feel so guilty?

She got the salad out of the refrigerator and put it on the table. "Brian," she yelled. "Come set the table!" She'd been foolish to think she might have a normal life, even for a little while. To think she might have a best friend, and to have that best friend spend the night. There was no way she was going to have Marcie over here while her father was home.

She knew better than that.

By the time she walked to school Thursday morning, she had figured out what she would say to Marcie. She'd say her father was home from his business trip early, and had a bad case of the flu.

The bell rang just as Jenny hurried into the classroom and sat down. Her stomach had an angry knot in it. She hated to lie, but she didn't know what else to do.

She looked across the aisle to Marcie's desk. It was empty.

Marcie was never late. She waited, almost holding her breath while Mrs. Neven took roll. Still Marcie didn't arrive.

For a minute, hope rose up in Jenny. Maybe Marcie would be absent tomorrow too -- and she wouldn't have to tell her the lie.

Then a worse thought hit her. What if Marcie DID show up? She'd already told Jenny she was bringing her sleeping bag and games with her to school -- and Jenny hadn't thought to tell Marcie her phone number.

The knot of anger was growing inside, spreading up until it almost choked her. It wasn't fair. This was her father's fault. If it wasn't for him, she wouldn't have to worry about things like this.

She was helpless. She had no control in her own life. Everything was falling apart and she could only watch while the pieces fell down around her.

Chapter 9

The Ceramic Blue Dinosaur

All the way home from school, Jenny tried to push her angry feelings down, to make them go away. When she walked into the house, the kitchen was a mess. There were pots and pans stacked all over the stove and countertops, and her mother was rolling out pie dough. "I took off work early. I decided to cook ahead for Dad's visit so we could relax while he's here."

"I thought he was only going to be here for six hours," Jenny said.

Her mother looked irritated. "I wanted to make something special. You know how he loves apple pie."

"I'll help clean up as soon as I put my books away," Jenny said.

Brian was sitting on the floor of his room, making a ramp for his matchbox cars. "Mom's crabby," he said. "She wouldn't let me clean the fishbowl, just because she was making pies."

Jenny took a deep breath, trying to stay calm. "Never mind, Brian. I'll help Mom finish up in the kitchen, and we'll clean the fishbowl later."

Jenny piled the books on her desk and went back down. She cleaned up the kitchen while her mother grumpily cut up apples, and then she went down to put a load of laundry in the washer. Brian followed her as she carried a pile of folded clothes to be put away. "Jenny, do you think Dad will be happy when he comes home tomorrow?"

Jenny didn't answer.

"The lady at that meeting said Dad might act funny for awhile."

"So what's new about that, Brian? We never know what to expect when Dad's around." Brian looked surprised at her sharp answer, but he didn't say anything else.

Jenny wished she could just be gone for the next few days. She felt tight inside, stretched like a rubberband about to snap. She moved the rocker over so she could hang the clean clothes in her closet.

As she touched the varnished arm of the chair, she remembered.

This was where her father used to sit when he read her bedtime stories. He'd had a beard then, and she used to kneel up to snuggle her cheek against its bristly softness when he turned the pages.

Goodnight, Moon.

That had been her favorite book. She had always loved looking for the little mouse on each page. She felt tears starting, and brushed them away impatiently.

"Brian, don't you have something better to do than to follow me around? You can help too, you know. Mom wants us to clean their bathroom." She handed him a can of foam cleaner. "Here, you do the sink while I scrub the tub."

"Why are we cleaning?" Brian asked. "Daddy's not company."

But it felt like it. It felt like some total stranger was coming to visit tomorrow, and Jenny was scared. She hoped with all her heart that Marcie would be absent again. She didn't want to lie to her, but she didn't want her here when her father was home.

Her father.

Those words sounded so strange. Who was her father? It seemed as if it had been months since Jenny had seen him.

She moved the soapdish to scrub the tile around the edge of the tub, and her hand stopped. She remembered kindergarten, when she'd made that soapdish. It was a ceramic blue dinosaur and she'd been so proud when she finished it.

Coming Home

It was a ceramic blue dinosaur and she'd been so proud when she finished it.

She'd given it to her father for Christmas that year.

She could see his strong hands now, turning the soapdish gently as he opened it. "Jenny," he'd said. "This blue dinosaur has personality. I'll keep it forever. I can tell you've got the family artistic streak." And he had hugged her.

It seemed like a long time since her father had hugged her, or paid any attention to her -- except to yell.

But he had kept the soapdish she'd given him. Her throat ached as she scrubbed the tile and put the soapdish back.

Brian had the sink full of foam when she turned around. "Brian! You're only supposed to use a little of that." She grabbed the can away from him. He didn't seem to mind.

He shaped the pile of suds into swoops and peaks. Jenny walked out of the room. That would keep him busy for a few minutes while she finished the other bathroom.

"Jenny?" Brian called. "Don't forget about Molly and Bubbles. Their bowl's really dirty."

"Okay, Brian." Jenny sighed. At least he had stopped drawing pictures of giant goldfish bowls. Maybe he had finally given up too.

Chapter 10

The Surprise Letter

When Jenny pushed open the classroom door the next morning she looked around the room, then let out a long breath. Marcie's desk was empty. She wouldn't have to lie.

She had enough on her mind, with her father coming home this afternoon. What would it be like to see him? She didn't want to think about it. Her feelings were all mixed up.

Jenny pushed down her growing sadness. She'd known better than to expect things to work out, so why did she feel so disappointed?

Had Marcie tried to get in touch with her? There were a lot of Turners in the phone book, just like there were a lot of Shields. Last night Jenny had tried five different numbers before she had finally given up. But maybe it hadn't been that important to Marcie. She was popular with all the kids; this was probably just another slumber party to her.

"Jenny Turner." Mrs. Neven's voice intruded into her thoughts, and she jumped. Now what? She'd turned in extra work to make up for last week.

Mrs. Neven walked over to her desk. "I have a note for you. Marcie Shield's little brother brought it."

Jenny took the envelope and went back to her seat. Several people watched her curiously. She set the envelope on the corner of her desk, unopened. At recess she carried the envelope to the far corner of the ballfield and sat down on the bench. Her hands felt warm and sweaty as she pulled the flap open. Marcie's handwriting scrawled across the page:

Jenny,

I'm still coming to spend the night with you! Had to take care of the kids for two days -- my mom's out of town. My aunt's coming this afternoon to take them to her house.

Meet you at 3:00 at Breyer's.

Marcie.

Jenny felt a heaviness in the pit of her stomach. She'd have to tell the lie after all. Once, just once, she'd like to have things work out right in her life.

She read the note again. Maybe Marcie would understand. She seemed different from the other kids Jenny knew.

But the more she thought about it, the more her doubts grew. Marcie wouldn't, couldn't understand. She came from a normal family.

She might as well give up on having Marcie as a friend. There was no way it could ever work.

When the bell rang at three, Jenny walked the three blocks to Breyer's. Sitting down on the steps out front, she waited.

She saw Marcie a few minutes later, loaded down with bundles. "You got my note!" she called out.

"I would have met you at school but I didn't want to have to explain everything to Mrs. Neven." Marcie made a face. "She would never understand Mom keeping me out of school to watch the kids."

Jenny's throat felt tight. She had to tell Marcie now, but she couldn't seem to get the words out.

Marcie set everything down and looked at her. "What's wrong? You're not mad, are you, Jenny? I tried to call yesterday, but there are so many Turners in the phone book. I didn't think of sending a note with Jamie until today."

Jenny's mouth felt dry. "You can't spend the night, Marcie. My father's ... sick."

Marcie looked pale.

Coming Home

Marcie set everything down and looked at her.
"What's wrong? You're not mad, are you, Jenny?"

"Oh no, Jenny. I'm sorry. Is he in the hospital?"

Why did Marcie look so upset? "It's not like that. He's got -- some kind of virus," Jenny said.

A strange look passed over Marcie's face and then was gone. "I'm glad it's nothing really bad." She sat down on top of the sleeping bag. "But I've got a problem. I don't have any place to go until tomorrow."

Jenny felt weak all over. "What do you mean? I'll walk you to the bus stop and you can just go back home."

Marcie shook her head. "The house is locked up and I don't have a key. My aunt took mine because she was going back with my brothers tomorrow morning."

"Can't you call her?"

Marcie looked embarrassed. "I know this sounds really dumb, but I don't know how to get in touch with her. She just moved and I don't have her phone number."

Jenny fought the panicky feeling that rose inside her. She was trapped again.

"Don't look so upset, Jenny. It's okay. I'll just come home with you and try to get my aunt's number from information. I won't bother your dad."

Marcie's words seemed to be coming from far away. Inside her head, Jenny was walking around and around, trying to find an answer to this problem.

She couldn't think of any. She'd have to take Marcie home with her.

Maybe her dad would be all right. Maybe he wouldn't drink, at least for these six hours. Maybe her dad...

The realization suddenly hit her.

Her dad.

Her dad was at the house right now.

Chapter 11

How Come Jenny's Acting So Weird?

Jenny's legs felt wobbly. She hoped they'd carry her the six blocks to home. Marcie kept talking, something about her mother and an early childhood conference.

Jenny couldn't concentrate on what Marcie was saying. Right now her father was probably sitting in the living room. She tried to think what he looked like. It had only been two weeks, but it seemed like two years. As hard as she tried, the image she remembered most was her father stretched out face down on the front lawn, drunk. She felt a sour taste at the back of her throat.

Marcie had stopped chattering and was watching her. "I'm sorry, Jenny. I never thought about something going wrong. I should have checked before showing up like this with all my stuff. Mom says I always put the cart before the horse."

She shifted the sleeping bag to her other arm. "I never get sick, so you don't 'have to worry about me catching the flu from your dad. I'll try to get my aunt's number as soon as we get to your house."

Maybe that would work, Jenny thought. If only her father would be in another part of the house when they got there.

She turned the corner, and stopped so quickly that Marcie ran into the back of her.

Her father was sitting on the front porch -- and he had a glass in his hand. Her stomach started to hurt.

I should have known, Jenny thought.

She walked straight ahead, her eyes focused on the ice cubes clinking in the glass that her father held. She was vaguely aware of Marcie following her up onto the porch.

"Jenny." Her father's voice was warm, welcoming. He sounded the way he used to when she was little. She stood as if frozen, a few feet away from him. She looked over at her mother, who was sitting

Coming Home

She walked straight ahead, her eyes focused on the ice cubes clinking in the glass that her father held.

on the wide porch railing. Next to her was a pitcher of lemonade.

Lemonade. That's what her father was drinking. Jenny felt something give way inside of her. She wanted so much to walk into his arms, to feel his hug again, but she couldn't seem to take those last few steps.

What if he had something else in the glass? She'd seen her father pour whiskey into coffee, juice, all sorts of drinks. Why not into lemonade?

Her father looked at her questioningly. There were so many feelings inside her. She was afraid of being hurt, of letting herself care again.

She realized she still hadn't said anything when her mother stood up. "You must be Marcie," she said.

Marcie. She'd forgotten about her for a moment. Marcie looked embarrassed. "I've been out of school for a couple of days, and I didn't let Jenny know I was still coming. I'm sorry you're sick, Mr. Turner. I'll try to call my aunt to get a ride home."

Her father looked puzzled. Jenny flushed. "We'd better take Marcie's stuff up to my room," she said. She realized as soon as she said it that it didn't make sense.

Why should she take Marcie's sleeping bag to her room when she wasn't going to spend the night?

Her head felt like it was going to explode. Quickly she picked up the box of games and started inside. "We'll stay upstairs for a while so you can rest, Dad." Her voice sounded trembly. Any minute she was going to cry.

She rushed into the house. Brian's voice trailed after her. "How come Jenny's acting so weird?"

Chapter 12

Playing by the Rules of the Game

Jenny sat down on her bed. She could feel how hot her face was. She must be bright red.

Marcie set the sleeping bag down on the floor. "Your dad seems to be feeling better. Flu's like that though. You feel better for awhile, and then you feel worse."

Jenny didn't say anything.

"Do you want me to call information and try to get my aunt's number?"

She wanted Marcie out as soon as possible. She had a feeling that something terrible was going to happen any minute. But she didn't want to go out of her bedroom. She wanted to stay here until she could calm down. "Let's play one of the games you brought." Her voice sounded shaky.

Marcie looked surprised. "Sure. Which one do you want to play. I've got Uno, Monopoly..."

Marcie paused. Out in the hall was the sound of running footsteps and then Brian pounded on the bedroom door. Jenny jumped up to open it.

"Can I come in? Mom said she wants to talk to Daddy, alone."

Brian looked over at Marcie, who was on the other side of the bed, sorting through games. "Do you think they'll yell at each other?" he asked Jenny in a whisper.

She frowned at him and shook her head.

In a louder voice he asked, "Can I stay and play too? Please?" Jenny felt anger stirring inside her. It wasn't fair. Why was she always the one who got caught in the middle? She didn't want to send Brian away; she knew how afraid he was of the fights between his mother and father. But she didn't want him to stay either. He could be a real pain, whining and getting upset when games didn't go his way.

Marcie looked up. "You can stay, Brian. I'm used to little brothers."

He looked pleased. "I'll be really good."

"We'll play charades," Marcie said. "The rules for that are simple. You act things out and try to guess what they are. For the first round, we'll act out people; real people, either living or dead."

She stood up. "See if you can guess who this is." She walked around the room with mincing steps, took an imaginary pair of glasses off her nose, squinted at them, wiped them with a corner of her shirt, and put them back on.

"Is it someone from our school?" Brian asked excitedly.

Marcie nodded, a grin on her face.

"Mr. Rooder!" Brian shouted. "He acts just like that! Now it's my turn."

"Okay, go ahead, Brian."

"The one I want to do isn't real people, but they live at our house."

"Marcie just told you they have to be real people for this round, Brian. That's the rule."

Brian scowled and sat down on the bed. "It's okay," Marcie said hastily. "Do the one you want, Brian."

Brian stood back up. "Marcie can't guess this, but I bet you can, Jenny." He leaned his head forward and began to open and close his mouth slowly.

Jenny sighed. Brian had a one-track mind lately. "Molly and Bubbles," she said.

There was a knock on the bedroom door. "Jenny, dinner in a few minutes. Come on down."

Jenny got up off the floor. "I'll be right back," she said to Marcie. She slipped out the bedroom door and closed it behind her. "Mom?"

Her mother, already halfway down the hall, turned around.

"Could Marcie and I eat in my bedroom?"

Her mother frowned. "Jenny, the whole point of this visit is for your father to have some time to spend with you."

Jenny was silent for a minute. "Mom, I don't want to be with Dad."

"Look, Jenny. I've tried to give you some time. I didn't make you go to the meetings. Now I wish I had. This is hard for all of us, but it won't help for you to try to avoid your father."

Jenny looked down at the blue and red design in the carpet. "Is he still drinking?" she asked.

"No, he's not," her mother said.

"Are you sure he didn't have anything in that lemonade?"

Her mother sighed. "I'm sure. I made the lemonade, and I poured it." She folded her arms. "Jenny, I know you've had lots of disappointments with your dad, but you've got to give him a chance.

Coming Home

"Look, Jenny. I've tried to give you some time."

And whether he makes it or not, you need to stop expecting the worst all the time. There are some things YOU can do to start making your life the way you'd like it to be."

My life would be the way I want it to be, if I knew for sure Dad would never drink again, Jenny wanted to say.

But she couldn't say it.

She looked down at the floor, carefully avoiding her mother's eyes. "What shall I say to Marcie?"

"Tell her she's welcome, of course. She can try to call her aunt after dinner if she still wants to go home."

Now what? How could she explain to Marcie why her father was at dinner when she'd already said he had flu? Even worse, what would they all talk about during the meal? She could feel her hands perspiring. "Okay," she said. "We'll be down in a few minutes."

Chapter 13

The Second Game of Charades

Brian looked upset when Jenny came back into the room. She wondered if he'd heard any of the conversation. "I'm not hungry for dinner yet," he said. "How come we're eating so early?"

"Because Daddy has to..." Jenny stopped in mid-sentence. She'd almost forgotten that Marcie didn't know what was happening. "Because Daddy needs to rest." She turned to Marcie. "My father...

feels better than he did this morning. He's going to eat dinner with us."

Brian looked puzzled, but he didn't say anything. He knows the rules for THIS game, Jenny thought. Don't say anything in front of someone who's not in the family.

When they came down, the table was set with a linen tablecloth and candles. They were having fried chicken and mashed potatoes; Jenny remembered how much her father had loved that dinner before....

Before.

Her mother looked flushed. "Jenny, could you put on the salad and vegetables? Your dad will be here in a minute."

But five minutes went by and her father didn't come in. Was he back in the family room looking for one of the bottles he used to keep hidden? Jenny felt a heavy weight in her stomach. Brian started to squirm. Her mother looked upset. "I'll go get Daddy. You can start dishing up, Jenny."

Brian had that look on his face; Jenny knew the tension was getting to him. She tried to distract him. "Brian, why don't you act out another charade while we're waiting?" she said.

He jumped up from his chair all too willingly. "Okay. See if you can guess." He began bobbing and weaving around the dining room table.

"Careful, Brian!" Jenny said. "You're going to break something." She could hear voices from the family room now. It was her mom and dad. Were they arguing or laughing? She couldn't tell.

Brian's voice was insistent now. "Watch! Watch this." He started to walk very carefully around the dining room, reaching out to catch his balance on each chair as he walked by.

The cold knot in Jenny's stomach moved slowly upwards as she realized what Brian was doing. He weaved to the side, knocking against the table. Marcie looked puzzled. "It looks like someone who's drunk," she said.

Jenny felt sick. I can't believe he's doing this, she thought.

The dining room door swung open and her mother and father walked into the room together, laughing. "I have a surprise --" Her father stopped in the middle of his sentence and stared at Brian.

Brian, intent on his performance, didn't see his father. He was in the kitchen now, staggering and mumbling and bumping into things. He started back. He had just reached the doorway when he looked up and saw his father.

His mouth fell open.

He jerked backward and his elbow hit the goldfish bowl on the counter. There was a loud crash as the bowl fell to the floor.

Jenny jumped up from her chair and bolted from the room. The last thing she saw was Molly and Bubbles flopping desperately on the kitchen floor.

Coming Home

He jerked backward and his elbow hit the goldfish bowl
on the counter.

Chapter 14

Jenny's Decision

Jenny sat on her bed and tried to stop shaking. She had known all along it wouldn't work. She looked down at her hands; they were steady, clenched together on her lap. All the shaking must be inside.

She closed her eyes and took deep breaths. The garden. She'd feel safe if she could just pretend she was in the garden. She tried to picture the waterfall and the daisies, but it wouldn't work. All she could think about were Molly and Bubbles flopping on the kitchen floor.

She heard a knock on the door but she ignored it. Marcie came into the room, gathered up her games and put them into the box. "The fish are okay," she said. "Your father saved them."

Saved them. Saved them. The words echoed in Jenny's ears. She should feel glad, but she just felt numb.

"It's his fault they needed saving in the first place," she said.

Marcie looked upset. "I don't know what your father's done but I think you should give him a chance."

Jenny felt her nails digging into her hands. "I've given him lots of chances. You don't know what it's been like these last few years."

"All right, all right!" Marcie said. "Just tell me where the phone is so I can call my aunt." She looked at Jenny. "Do you have any idea what I would do, to be able to talk to my father?"

Jenny sat very still on the bed. "Why can't you talk to your father?"

"Because my father's dead. He died four years ago." Marcie walked out of the room.

Jenny felt the slam of her words like a fist punching. She'd been so sure Marcie had a normal family. But then -- what was a normal family?

Jenny got up off the bed and went out into the hall. Marcie was standing there; she looked like she'd been crying. "Could you please tell me where the phone is? I want to call my aunt."

"It's downstairs at the end of the hall," Jenny said. "I'll show you."

She swallowed. "I'm sorry, Marcie. I didn't know." She led Marcie down the stairs to the little alcove where the phone was.

She saw her father then. He was in the family room and Brian was with him. She wanted to turn and go back upstairs before he saw her, but she couldn't seem to move.

They were intent on watching something just out of sight in the corner of the room. Jenny took a step forward. She caught a glimpse of a hazy bluish light, and moving shapes. She took another step.

An aquarium. A real aquarium.

Brian looked so happy, he was practically dancing with excitement. "When did you get this, Daddy? Mom said we couldn't afford it."

"We got it on the way home this afternoon. Your mom and I talked and decided this was important. I finished setting it up right before dinner; that's why I was late coming in."

Brian pressed his nose against the glass. "Look at Molly and Bubbles. They love that little diver. See, Molly keeps bumping it with her nose. She always wanted to have a diver that made bubbles."

As Jenny watched, her father handed Brian a wispy green plant. "Here, you can plant this. Just poke it down into the rocks at the bottom."

"All right!" Brian's face was bright with happiness as he clutched the plant in his hand and stretched his arm over the top of the aquarium. He bit his lip as he struggled to get the plant to stay in place. He started to laugh. "Molly and Bubbles think I'm coming in with them. Look how they're nibbling my fingers." Jenny couldn't help smiling as she watched Brian's joy.

He had forgotten to roll up his sleeve and when he pulled his arm back out, a puddle of water dripped onto the floor. He didn't even notice. He looked up at his father and his smile lit up his whole face. "You even got blue rocks. How did you know they like blue the best?"

Brian hugged him. "I always knew you'd get the aquarium sometime."

Jenny took a step backwards, almost bumping into Marcie. Brian had trusted. Why couldn't she?

"Your father made me promise not to tell you about the aquarium," Marcie said. "He wanted you to come down and see for yourself when you were ready."

Was she ready? She remembered her mother's words. "I know it's hard but you have to give him a chance and start building trust."

But he'd broken so many promises. How could she ever believe in him again?

She stood there uncertainly. Maybe she could start by trusting other people. Marcie wanted to be her friend. She took a deep breath. "Marcie, don't call your aunt."

Marcie looked at her. "Are you sure?"

"I'm... sure. Stay here and spend the night."

Marcie didn't say anything for a minute. Then she grinned. "Okay," she said. "Sounds good to me."

Brian looked up then and saw her. "Jenny!" he shouted. He rushed over and grabbed her arm. "Come look. Daddy kept his promise."

Her heart started pounding. "Let go, Brian. You're getting me all wet." But she let herself be dragged over to the aquarium.

"You can help us, Jenny. We're putting in the plants." Brian picked up a dripping piece of seaweed and shoved it into her hand. "Here. You do this one."

The plant was cold and soggy. She stood there with water trickling down her arm. Her father was watching her, and she could see the pain in his eyes. "It's hard work to keep an aquarium running right, Jenny. Will you help us?"

"Please, Jenny," Brian said. "If we all do it together it will be lots easier."

She hesitated. She looked over at Marcie, still standing in the doorway. Marcie was smiling but there was a sadness in her eyes. Jenny knew she was thinking about her own father.

Jenny took a deep breath and looked up. "Okay," she said. "I'll help."

Her father put his hand gently on her shoulder. "Thank you," he said. Jenny bit her lip to hold back her tears. It had been so long since she'd felt the gentleness of her father's touch.

Brian grabbed her hand. "Really, truly, Jenny? You really, truly promise?"

Jenny smiled. "I really, truly promise," she said.

"I really, truly promise," she said.

Child's page

What should you do if you're reading this book and you think your mother or father or someone else living in your home is an alcoholic? It's scary to tell someone, but it's also scary not to have anyone to talk to about it.

The best thing to do is to think of an adult that you can trust. It may be someone in your family. It may be your teacher, or your doctor, or your best friend's mother or father. Tell them your concern and ask for their help. If that person doesn't seem to understand or believe you, then tell another adult. Someone will listen! And you won't feel so alone anymore.

Book List

A Workbook For Healing, Patty Mc Connell
Harper & Row

Adult Children of Alcoholics, Janet G. Woititz,
Ed. D. Health Communications, Inc

After the Tears, Jane Middleton-Moz, & Lorie Dwinnell
Health Communications, Inc

Children of Alcoholics: A Survivor's Manual, Judith
S. Seixas & Geraldine Youcha,
Harper & Row

It Will Never Happen To Me,
Claudia Black, PhD, MSW,
M.A.C. Printing & Publications Division

My Dad Loves Me, My Dad Has A Disease, Claudia
Black, PhD, MSW,
M.A.C. Printing & Publications Division

Repeat After Me, Claudia Black, PhD, MSW,
M.A.C. Printing & Publications Division

Struggle For Intimacy, G. Woititz, Ed. D.
Health Communications, Inc

Resources

Alcoholics Anonymous National Headquarters
General Service Office
PO Box 459
Grand Central Station
New York, NY 10163
(212) 686-1100

Al-Anon National Headquarters
Alateen
PO Box 862
Midtown Station
New York, NY 10018 - 0862
(212) 302-7240

Adult Children of Alcoholics
Central Service Board
PO Box 35623
Los Angeles, CA 90035
(213) 464-4423

THE GLEN ABBEY PROMISE

Please send me the following books. It is my understanding
that if I am not completely satisfied with any book, I may return
it within 30 days for a full refund. Thank you.

Order Toll Free 1-800-782-2239

Quantity	Title of Book	Price	Total Amt
	A Reference Guide to the Big Book of Alcoholics Anonymous ISBN 0-934125-01-5	$9.95	
	Coming Home A healing story for Adult Children of Alcoholics ISBN 0-934125-06-6	$7.95	
	A Year to Remember 52 Contemplative Messages on 12 Step Recovery and Christianity ISBN 0-934125-05-8	$7.95	
	A A The Way It Began The Untold Story ISBN 0-934125-02-3	$8.95	
	Stepping Stones to Recovery Spiritual Insights into Recovery Compiled from the membership of Alcoholics Anonymous over the past 50 years ISBN 0-934125-04-X	$8.95	
	Total number of books ordered	Subtotal =	
		Postage $1.00/book	
		Total Order	

[ ] Check enclosed with order
[ ] Please charge to my credit card number
[ ] Visa   [ ] MasterCard
Number _____

Expiry Date _____

Signature _____

Name _____

Company Name _____

Address _____

_____

Phone Number _____

Glen Abbey Books Po Box 19762, Seattle, WA. 98109

Peggy King Anderson

Coming Home is Peggy's first book. She has, however, been writing inspirational stories for children and adults since 1980 and has been published in several magazines, including *Highlights for Children, Pockets, Wee Wisdom, Junior Trails*, and many more. Peggy is a mother of teenage children and she is particularly concerned with the serious problems young people face today.

"Childhood isn't always fun", she says. "I am impressed with the courage and hope I see in so many of our young people. With the support of friends and a few understanding adults, they are learning to cope, like Jenny and Brian - the two main characters in *Coming Home* - and growing stronger as they do."

Peggy teaches creative writing to both children and adults at schools, libraries and writers work shops, throughout. Many of her stories have won prizes in the past and she will teach at the "Highlights Writer's Workshop" in Chattaqua, New York, in Summer of 1988.

Coming Home is the first of the *Mending Memories* books. These stories are written to help Adult Children of Alcoholics deal with feelings from their past.